VICTORIA'S NATIONAL PARKS

Photography by Ken Stepnell
Text by Dalys Newman

WOOLLAHRA

PRECEDING PAGE: Majestic old red gums line the foreshore of Hattah Lakes in the Hattah Kulkyne National Park.

ABOVE: Gabo Island, 500 metres off the wilderness coast of Croajingolong National Park in Bass Strait, covers an area of 154 hectares. The light station here was constructed in 1862, prompted by disastrous shipwrecks in the area. The light tower is constructed from pink granite which was cut locally and is one of the tallest and most elegant light towers in Australia.

BELOW LEFT: Set in some of Victoria's most beautiful Lakeland country, Croajingolong National Park preserves the bays, islands and lakes of Mallacoota Inlet. Stretching along 100 kilometres of coastline, the park is home to more than 70 native orchid and wildflower species as well as at least 250 different species of birds.

BELOW RIGHT: Bird's eye view of the Point Hicks Lighthouse in the Croajingolong National Park. Remote Point Hicks, on the coast of far east Gippsland, was the first part of Australia seen by Captain Cook in 1770. The lighthouse, completed in 1890, has an imposing concrete tower and a cast iron spiral staircase.

OPPOSITE: A series of straight basalt columns, resembling organ pipes, is the central feature of the Organ Pipes National Park. These 'pipes' were formed about a million years ago when a massive lava flow spread over the plains from nearby volcanic hills.

OPPOSITE: A small bridge is suspended over a verdant valley of tree ferns in the Tarra-Bulga National Park in South Gippsland. The 1625 hectare park contains cool temperate rainforest and is renowned for its giant mountain ash trees, fern gullies and ancient myrtle beeches.

ABOVE: Warm temperate rainforest grows in the gullies of the Lind National Park, named after Sir Albert Lind, the Minister for Lands who was responsible for the reservation of five of Victoria's national parks.

CENTRE: Majestic old ferns frame the deep red flowers of a Gippsland waratah in a warm temperate rainforest area in the Lind National Park. Rainforests provide one of the richest habitats for primitive flowering plants. The familiar plants of the Australian bush—hakeas, grevilleas, banksias and eucalypts—are thought to have evolved from the ancient forests.

RIGHT: Massed tree ferns in the Tarra-Bulga National Park. In the temperate rainforest, where palms generally do not grow, their place in the forest structure is taken by tree ferns.

ABOVE: Ancient tree ferns in the Tarra-Bulga National Park. Many small ferns soften the landscape of temperate forests, with probably the greatest number of species being found in the fern gullies of the Victorian forests.

ABOVE RIGHT: Fishing off Ninety Mile Beach in The Lakes National Park. The Gippsland Lakes, one of Australia's major waterways, are protected from the ocean by the high dune system of this stretch of beach.

RIGHT: Aerial view of Ninety Mile Beach and the Gippsland Lakes. This area was once part of a large bay, long since enclosed by a sand barrier transported by ocean currents. Fringed by the waters of Lake Victoria and Lake Reeve, The Lakes National Park, covering 2390 hectares, conserves low-lying woodland and coastal heath, together with an abundance of wildlife.

OPPOSITE: Fun in the snow at the Mount Buffalo National Park, one of Victoria's most popular parks.

OVERLEAF: The Horn, a feature of the Mount Buffalo National Park, north-east of Melbourne. Granite tors, rounded boulders and massive rock formations make up the landscape of this park.

ABOVE: Towering above the Ovens Valley, the high plateau of the Mount Buffalo National Park looks out over the spectacular Victorian Alps. The sheer cliffs and eroded granite outcrops of this landscape resisted attempts at exploration for many years. First reserved in 1898, the 31 000 hectare park contains vegetation and fauna adapted to extremes of weather.

ABOVE RIGHT: Wildflowers create a pretty foreground to stunning views over the Victorian Alps from the Great Alpine Road near Hotham Heights.

CENTRE RIGHT: Wallace's Hut, an historic cattleman's snow shelter, is near Falls Creek in the heart of the Alpine National Park. Classified under the National Trust, the hut was built by the Wallace brothers in 1889 from slabs of snowgum. It was taken over as a worker's hut in the 1930s and now serves as a refuge nestled in the wild country.

RIGHT: The largest river red gum forest in Australia is to be found in the Barmah State Park and Barmah State Forest. These majestic trees, some of which are over 500 years old, can reach 45 metres in height with gnarled, rock-like trunks.

LEFT: Victoria's largest stand of cool temperate rainforest, dominated by southern sassafras and black oliveberry, is found in the Errinundra National Park. Wet eucalypt forests of shining gum and cut-tail are found on the plateau, often over an understorey of rainforest, creating a mixed forest vegetation which is rare in Australia. There are 15 different ecological vegetation classes in the park, supporting more than 600 plant species, including the tree form of the mountain plum pine, unique to this area. Errinundra Plateau is the source of seven rivers that flow into Bass Strait or become part of the Snowy River system.

BELOW: Billy Goat Bend and the Amphitheatre, a semi-circular cliff in the Mitchell River National Park. The park, which contains some of Gippsland's best forest country, is notable for the Den of Nargun, a shallow cave beneath a small waterfall, that is part of Aboriginal legend. The Nargun, a beast that was all stone except for its breast, hands and arms, would drag unwary travellers into his den, forcing their weapons to be turned back on themselves.

OPPOSITE AND BELOW: Cool temperate rainforest at Melba Gully, near Lavers Hill in the Otway National Park. The gully is densely clothed in myrtle beech, blackwood and tree ferns with a lush understorey of mosses and ferns. An interpretive walk explores the forest surrounds. This rainforest area, characterised by a single tree species in the canopy and several species at lower levels, is one of the wettest places in Victoria.

RIGHT: Lake Surprise, a 700 metre long spring-fed lake in the Mount Eccles National Park. Many thousands of years ago, volcanic eruptions formed Mount Eccles and the surrounding landscape. Today, the three main craters are filled with the lake and the once red-hot lava is covered with heathland and manna gum forest.

BELOW RIGHT AND BOTTOM RIGHT: The Snowy River forms the backbone of the Snowy River National Park in eastern Victoria. MacKillops Bridge (below right) is one of the few places that provides access to this remote wilderness area by conventional vehicle. The Snowy River is a popular spot for canoeing and rafting but it is extremely dangerous in flood, often rising and falling up to 9 metres overnight.

OPPOSITE: Sandy stretches line the Tidal River that flows into Norman Bay in the Wilsons Promontory National Park. This area, 30 kilometres inside the park boundary, is the focus for tourism and recreation with an Information Centre, some 450 camping and caravan sites, self-contained flats, lodges, motor huts and shops.

ABOVE: Cleft Island, Wilsons Promontory National Park. The offshore islands here provide roosting and breeding sites for sea birds, including a large number of short-tailed shearwaters.

BELOW: Built in 1859, this dramatic granite light tower and keeper's residence was the first permanent building on Wilsons Promontory. Perched on a small peninsula jutting into the turbulent seas of Bass Strait, this is the most southerly lighthouse on mainland Victoria. The building stands 19 metres high with an elevation of 117 metres above sea level and the light has a range of 18 nautical miles.

ABOVE: Refuge Cove, one of the many sheltered coves in Wilsons Promontory National Park. The coastline of this park is characterised by expansive intertidal mudflats, sandy beaches and coves, broken by prominent headlands and sheer granite cliffs in the south.

CENTRE: One of the State's largest and most popular parks, Wilsons Promontory National Park is at the southernmost point of the Australian mainland. Its 130 kilometre coastline, with its sweeping white beaches, is framed by granite headlands, tall forests, fern gullies and salt marshes. The park contains a wealth of wildlife and conserves the largest coastal wilderness area in Victoria.

LEFT: Rock formations of Pillar Point in the Wilsons Promontory National Park. The promontory is the northern tip of a huge granite mass that extends to Tasmania. Erosion of the granite has created the spectacular rugged landscape that is in evidence today.

OPPOSITE: A beacon to shipping and beachcombers—the lighthouse on Cape Schanck in the Mornington Peninsula National Park.

LEFT AND BELOW: The Point Nepean section of the Mornington Peninsula National Park covers 311 hectares of historic features, outstanding coastal scenery and panoramic views of Bass Strait, the Rip and Port Phillip Bay. Since the 1850s Point Nepean has been off limits to the general public, first as a quarantine station and then as a military fortification. The quarantine station was established in 1852 to protect the colony of Melbourne from ship-borne diseases. The area now protects the remains of military fortifications from the 1880s, World War I and World War II. Point Nepean is also home to a diverse range of wildlife including the white-footed dunnart, the southern brown bandicoot and the New Holland mouse. Its intertidal zone provides an important environment for shellfish and marine invertebrates.

ABOVE LEFT AND CENTRE LEFT: Covering 2686 hectares, the Mornington Peninsula National Park protects diverse coastal environments ranging from basalt cliffs to native bushland and roaring surf. The 40 kilometres of windswept coastline and hinterland separates the turbulent waters of Bass Strait from the more placid waters of Port Phillip Bay. Behind the cliffs and sand dunes the dominant plant is the hardy coast tea tree and banksias, sheoaks and eucalypts grow in sheltered pockets.

LEFT: Birdlife on the old jetty in the Point Cook National Park, a popular destination for birdwatchers. Visiting migratory birds move between the wetlands and saltmarsh and Point Cook, the beach sand flats and Cheetham Wetlands. The endangered orange-bellied parrot has been seen in this park and the double-banded plover migrates here from New Zealand during the winter.

ABOVE: The historic bluestone homestead in the Point Cook National Park. The park was once part of a huge pastoral estate belonging to the Chirnside family and their homestead, stables and outbuildings, constructed in 1857, are now classified by the National Trust.

TOP LEFT: The Stony Creek Picnic Area in the Brisbane Ranges National Park, less than an hour's drive from Melbourne. The park is rich in flora and fauna with the greatest density of koalas in Victoria. It also contains 619 plant species that represent nearly a quarter of the State's native flora.

LEFT: Spring wildflowers brighten the campsite at the Little Desert National Park. The landscape here is arid due to a rainfall range between 400 and 600 millimetres a year. There are extensive heathlands in the eastern part of the park and woodlands and clay flats in the west.

LEFT AND BOTTOM LEFT: Wyperfield National Park contains some interesting relics of early farming days, such as an old wooden dog leg fence (left) and a whim (bottom left) that was used by early settlers for lifting water for their needs. James Clow was the first European to establish a pastoral run in this flat, semi-arid north-western corner of Victoria in 1847. Other settlers followed, clearing the mallee for grazing and wheat growing. The area was proclaimed a national park in 1921, its central feature being a chain of lake beds connected by the Outlet Creek, the northern extension of the Wimmera River.

OPPOSITE: Erskine Falls cascade over one of the highest drops of the Otway Ranges in the 22 000 hectare Angahook-Lorne State Park. Steep timbered ridges, fern gullies, waterfalls and a coastal area of tall cliffs, coves and sandy beaches make up the landscape of this park. There were eight shipwrecks off the coast here. A grave site and artefacts of one of them is visible in the rock shelf at low tide.

OPPOSITE: Enjoying the spectacular Hopetoun Falls in the Otway Ranges.

TOP RIGHT: The Cape Otway Lighthouse at the northern end of the Eye of the Needle in the Cape Otway National Park was the oldest operational lighthouse with unbroken service on the mainland Australian Coast until it was decommissioned in 1994. The light was first lit in 1848. First whale oil and then kerosene was used to keep the light burning. Later, diesel generators provided electricity, before 240 volt power was connected. In 1994, the introduction of satellite navigation systems caused the 'old light' to be turned off and replaced with a low-powered solar beacon positioned in front of the original tower.

RIGHT: The Angahook-Lorne State Park forms a breathtaking backdrop to the renowned Great Ocean Road. Forests of blue gum, messmate and mountain gum cover the hills and gullies of this park. In spring there are masses of wildflowers and orchids on the heathlands in the north of the park.

RIGHT: Dense bush, a rugged cliff face and an idyllic campsite at the entrance to the Cumberland River and Gorge in the Angahook-Lorne State Park.

BOTTOM RIGHT: Massive sand dunes at the Discovery Bay Coastal Park. The majestic 50 kilometre sweep of coastline here offers ocean beaches, Aboriginal middens and coastal lakes and is an important habitat for the endangered hooded plover and many other waders migrating from overseas. Discovery Bay was named by Lieutenant Grant in 1800 during a voyage along the south-western coast of what is now Victoria.

OVERLEAF: The Port Campbell National Park encompasses more than 2400 hectares of rugged scenic coastline between Peterborough and Princetown. The spectacular coastline is a result of the waves of the stormy Southern Ocean pounding the limestone plateau over millions of years.

ABOVE AND OPPOSITE: The Twelve Apostles in the Port Campbell National Park have been sculpted by surging seas and howling southerly storms blowing in from the freezing waters above Antarctica. Towering as high as 60 metres above the turbulent waters, these narrow pillars of rocks are in a constant state of change as the ocean wears away at their soft limestone foundations and in time will topple down into the churning waters below.

BELOW LEFT AND BELOW RIGHT: Loch Ard Gorge in the Port Campbell National Park, site of the shipwreck of the *Loch Ard*, one of the many sailing vessels that foundered in the treacherous surf and hidden rocks of the Port Campbell coastline. Grotesque stalactites fringe the Eva Carmichael Cave (below left), named after a shipwreck survivor, adding to the foreboding atmosphere of the gorge (below right). There are treacherous undertows and cross currents in the water and the beach is constantly swept by noisy, eerie winds.

OPPOSITE: Aerial view of the many small islands that make up the Bay of Islands Coastal Park which stretches from Peterborough almost to Warrnambool in a 32 kilometre long strip. The park is also renowned for its variety of rare and threatened flora and fauna species and some fascinating post-colonial and Aboriginal history.

ABOVE AND CENTRE RIGHT: Tower Hill, in the Tower Hill State Game Reserve, was formed at least 30 000 years ago when a violent explosion created a funnel-shaped crater, now filled by a lake and the islands seen today. Artefacts found in the volcanic ash layers show that Aborigines were living in the area at the time of eruption. Declared Victoria's first National Park in 1892, the area was made into a State Game Reserve in 1961. A massive revegetation programme was implemented, with more than 300 000 indigenous trees being planted.

BOTTOM RIGHT: Often called Victoria's Uluru, the spectacular Mount Arapiles rises from the Wimmera Plains to form part of the Mount Arapiles–Tooan State Park. The mountain is of world renown as a top rock-climbing area.

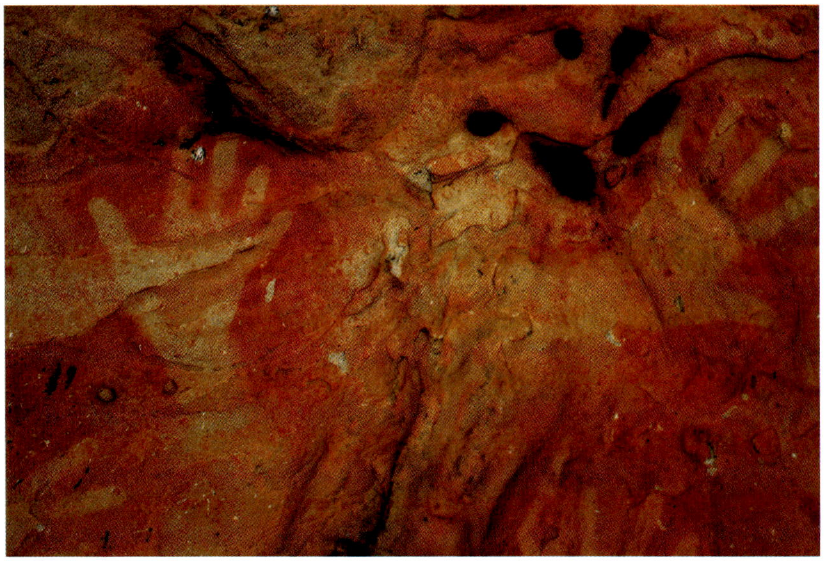

ABOVE: The Balconies (previously known as the Jaws of Death) provide an excellent vantage point for the intrepid sightseer in the Grampians National Park. Declared in 1984, the 167 000 hectare park is renowned for its rugged mountain ranges and stunning wildflower displays. It is home for almost a third of Victoria's plant species.

CENTRE LEFT: Mount Abrupt towers over the surrounding landscape in the Grampians National Park. The region, forming the westernmost heights of the Great Dividing Range, is comprised of folded and weathered sandstone. One of the features of this park is the stunning spring wildflower display when the heathlands come to life in a burst of colour.

LEFT: Aboriginal paintings in the Cave of Hands in the Grampians. Aboriginal occupation of this area dates back beyond 5000 years with the Jardwadjali and Djab Wurrung people inhabiting the mountains and valleys. Most of the rock art sites in south-east Australia are to be found in this area.

OPPOSITE: The lookout point on Wonderland Range in the Grampians provides panoramic views of the national park. Three sizable lakes and countless streams and waterfalls are included within the park boundaries.

LEFT: Looking into the Grand Canyon in the Grampians. This steep, narrow gorge has been deeply etched by rain and chemical action. The Grampians National Park features many striking landforms including the Balconies near Halls Gap, the Broken Falls on the Mackenzie River and the tough upthrust ridges of the Serra Range. Mt William rises to 1168 metres in the east and many summits in the park exceed 800 metres.

BELOW: The peaceful Glenelg River is at the heart of the 27 300 hectare Lower Glenelg National Park in the south-west corner of Victoria. Canoeing, fishing and bushwalking are popular activities in this park and the river has carved a spectacular 50 metre gorge through limestone along the last part of its meandering 400 kilometre journey to the sea. River erosion has also carved some remarkable caves and there is a rich variety of flora and fauna in the park.